My Emotional Martial Arts Coloring Journal

Volume 1

Emotional Martial Arts™

Coloring Journal
Volume 1

Based on the teachings of
Howard E. Richmond, MD

Elana Cohen Richmond
Deborah Louise Brown

COLORING JOURNALS FOR HEALTHY LIVING

Copyright © 2015
by Elana Cohen Richmond and Deborah Louise Brown

Published by Brave Maven Press

Illustrations and design © 2015 Deborah Louise Brown

All rights reserved. No part of this book may be reproduced or transmitted in any form or by any means, including but not limited to information storage and retrieval systems, electronic, mechanical, photocopy, recording, etc. without written permission from the copyright holder.

Disclaimer: While journaling prompts and guided meditations are excellent tools for helping to relieve stress and encourage creativity and life balance, they are not substitutes for medical advice or professional counseling and support for depression or other conditions you might be experiencing. Please seek assistance if you need it.

Namaste ... Elana and Deborah

ColoringJournalsforHealthyLiving.com

ISBN: 978-1-517631-19-2

My hope is that you experience your daily activity as an expression of your spiritual essence.

~ Elana

FOREWORD

Emotional Martial Arts™ (EMA) is the practice of becoming keenly aware in the now, when we are in "reaction mode," of how emotions drive our perception, shape our reality and trigger reflexive thoughts and behaviors that can cause harm.

Applying the "black-belt" tools of EMA (recognizing and validating hidden emotions, cultivating compassion and releasing limiting judgments) realigns body, mind and spirit to increase our capacity for joy, creativity, empowerment, and ultimately, inner peace.

As with any discipline, the more familiar and fluent we become with EMA, the doors of perception will shift, widen, and open you up to a journey of exploration of you!

The EMA interactive coloring journal invites you to become more self-aware in the practice of emotional attunement, emotional release and letting go of conditioned beliefs!

Welcome to integrating your Self into a more present being of light, love and truth.

Inner Peace: Let's Wage It!

Dr. H

Howard E. Richmond, MD

DEAR CONSCIOUSLY SEEKING FRIEND,

Howard E. Richmond, MD, founder of Emotional Martial Arts™ (EMA), has been a transformational psychiatrist for over 25 years. Patients and friends call him Dr. H ... I call him my loving husband and best friend. I am truly grateful for the opportunity to learn from him, as well. And, I get the gift of observing how his wisdom and guidance shows people how to break out of the prisons of their stories. I get to watch them as they take, at first, unsure small steps and then begin to walk more and more confidently into cultivating these principles; and to see how the tools of Emotional Martial Arts™ help them create lives of conscious awareness and find appreciation even for the events that are a challenge.

Dr. H has developed a series of lessons that incorporate his years of training, experience and intuition for helping others make changes in their lives. As his partner in bringing EMA to the world, I have been able to not only support and facilitate opportunities for teaching but I have the blessing of being the number one student of the EMA principles. This has made me a better listener, and given me more presence when people share their struggles and breakthroughs with me. It has also helped me to be more aware of the blind spots in my life and in interactions with others – helping me to identify more quickly when I am coming from "reaction mode" so I can move into using these transformational tools! I can tell you, it's often not fun in the midst of it... afterwards when I have moved through the trigger like a ninja warrior, I feel empowered, full of even more love and joy and incredible gratitude!

Whether you join us at our Emotional Martial Arts™ events or not, this coloring journal is designed as a fun tool: to be an outlet for processing; to activate your brain centers that don't require thinking or "figuring it out;" to document your journey; and to offer some guidance and references along the way. Dr H teaches us with story-telling and humor, so let's just add a little more fun to the process!! Why not?!

Enjoy the book and we'll meet you in the healing field!

Namaste,

Elana

Join our list at http://HowardRichmondMD.com for news and updates about **Emotional Martial Arts**™ events and upcoming journals.

COLORING IMPLEMENTS

When I picked up my first "coloring book for adults" I had all kinds of angst about how to proceed! When I was little, a fist full of Crayola crayons served me so well ... but I'm a grown up. Now what?

Happily, I discovered that all you really need to get started are markers, colored pencils, gel pens, or pens! There are no rules ...

I did a quick search online to discover the "best" brands for colored pencils. Prismacolor made the top of the list, and I bought my first set of twenty colors. Delightful.

I then learned that what I really like is the effects I can create with a combination of colored pencils and markers, with gel pens thrown in for good measure. My Papermate Flair collection is extensive, with vibrant colors ranging from primary colors through tropical. The medium point is nice for tight spaces and you don't have to sharpen markers like you do pencils.

Deborah

My Favorites (even layered on top of each other):

Prismacolor – Artist-quality colored pencils designed for every level of expertise. Colors are easily blended, slow to wear and waterproof. Thick leads resist breakage. Soft, thick cores create a smooth color laydown for superior blending and shading. High-quality pigments deliver rich color saturation. *(as described on Amazon.com)*

Papermate Flair – The world's classic felt tip writing instrument lets you express yourself with true style and color. Quick-drying, water-based ink prevents smearing, and your writing won't bleed through paper. Available in 26 colors with medium tip and 8 colors with ultra fine tip. Love the Tropicals! *(as described on Amazon.com)*

Crayola Twistables – Special Effects! Metallic Crayons provide shimmering effects on white and dark paper *(or the black areas of our designs)*. Super Bright Neon Crayons for art with an edge! Crayons never need to be sharpened. *(as described on Amazon.com)*

AND THOUSANDS OF OTHER OPTIONS ... see **ColoringJournalsforHealthyLiving.com** for more ways to color and create.

BENEFITS OF COLORING & JOURNALING

Psychologists report that coloring engages multiple parts of our brains. This creates new synapses (*we're doing something new and fun*) and also balances right (*creative*) and left (*linear*) cerebral processes.

Journaling lets us focus through writing and enables us to hear our own inner guidance, especially by responding to journal-prompts about our feelings, visions and dreams . It also puts stories and beliefs that can obscure our vision down on paper where we can better look at them – and even move through them to a new insight.

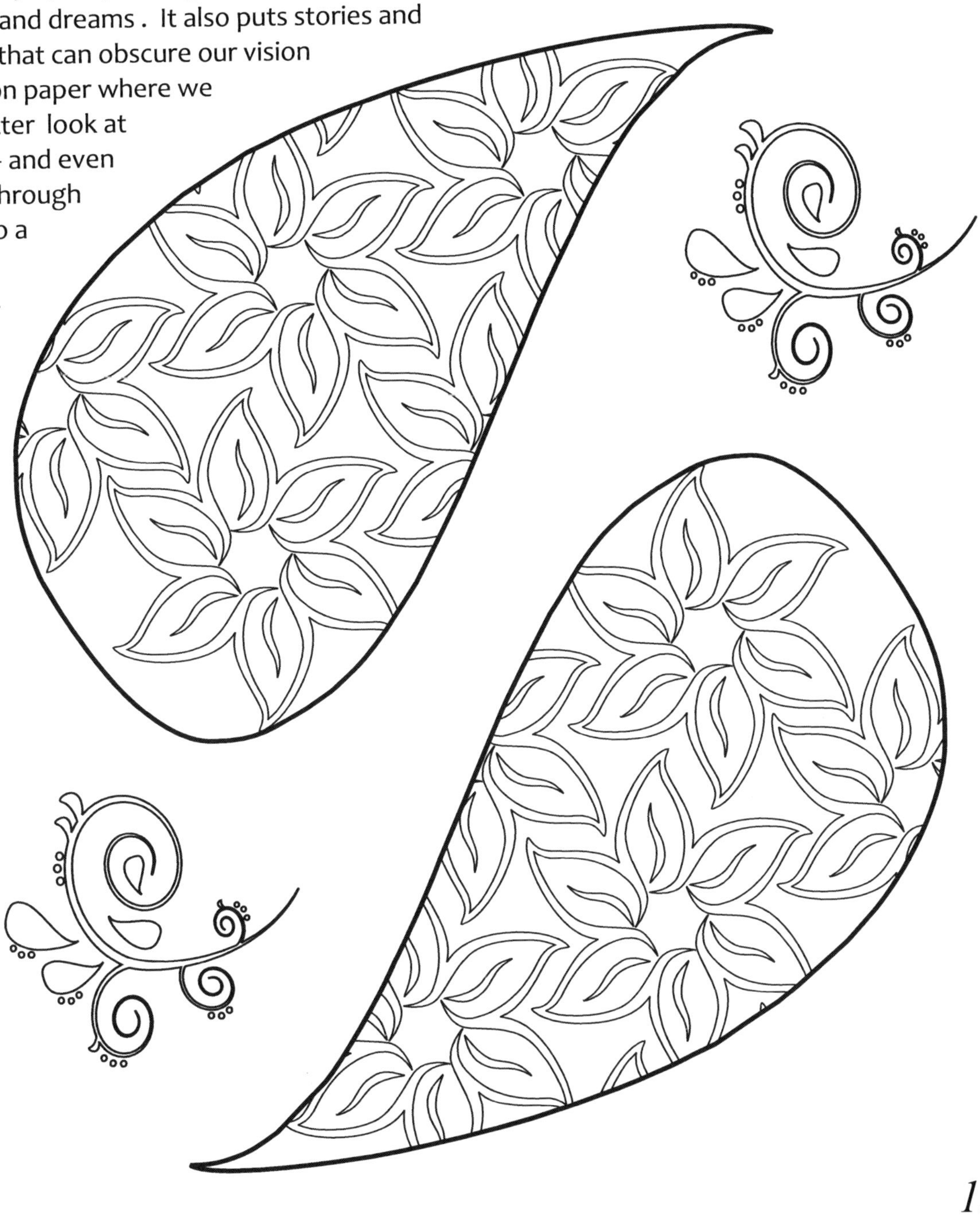

HOW TO USE THIS COLORING JOURNAL WORKBOOK

Make It Your Own! By coloring the images and/or using different colored pens/pencils in the journaling or listing sections, you infuse each page with your unique and personal energy.

Experiment! Try out colors combinations you don't usually see together – or different shades of the same color next to each other. Feel free to use one coloring tool throughout, like gel-pens or crayons – or mix-and-match coloring tools on one image that has both wide sections (for crayons) and smaller/thinner sections (for colored pencils or markers). Be precise and focused – or go wild and try out bolder strokes or shading styles.

To prevent marker bleed-through, place a piece of cardboard behind the page you are coloring.

Color Your Heart Out! There is no right or preferred way to color or journal – there's only YOUR way because YOU are evolving and changing every day!

Go through the Book Page by Page or Skip Around! Notice where your attention is drawn today – to a mandala, an animal image, an abstract, a nature scene, a puzzle-style drawing? What style of image could help you get focused today? What would be fun or challenging to color or write about? Which section could help you gain clarity on a current life-issue or question – or let you "escape" your problems by coloring and just having fun?

Find Time – Try to find time to journal and focus week by week, even if you have to make a "coloring date" with yourself! Life seems to "just happen" while we're busy living it – but we can feel and even track our personal progress when we take time to pause and reflect. Use the coloring pages to focus and explore, and the journaling pages to reflect and plan. *You could work on coloring one page for a whole month to practice mindfulness and "being in the moment."*

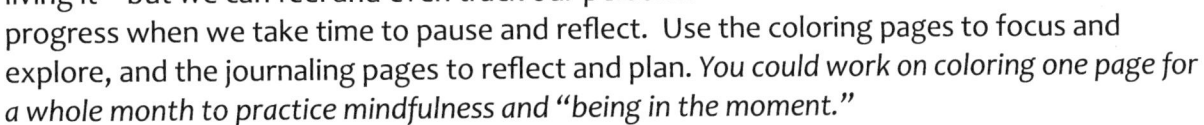

Our Exclusive Emotional Martial Arts ™ Meditations – We've created these to help you relieve stress and relax, focus and visualize, whenever you want. Find links to our guided meditations throughout our coloring journals and calendars – and also on our Resources pages. You can listen to these "inner journeys" before you color or journal... while you're coloring... or anytime for fun!

When we wage inner peace, we no longer wage inner – or outer – war.

~ Howard E. Richmond, MD

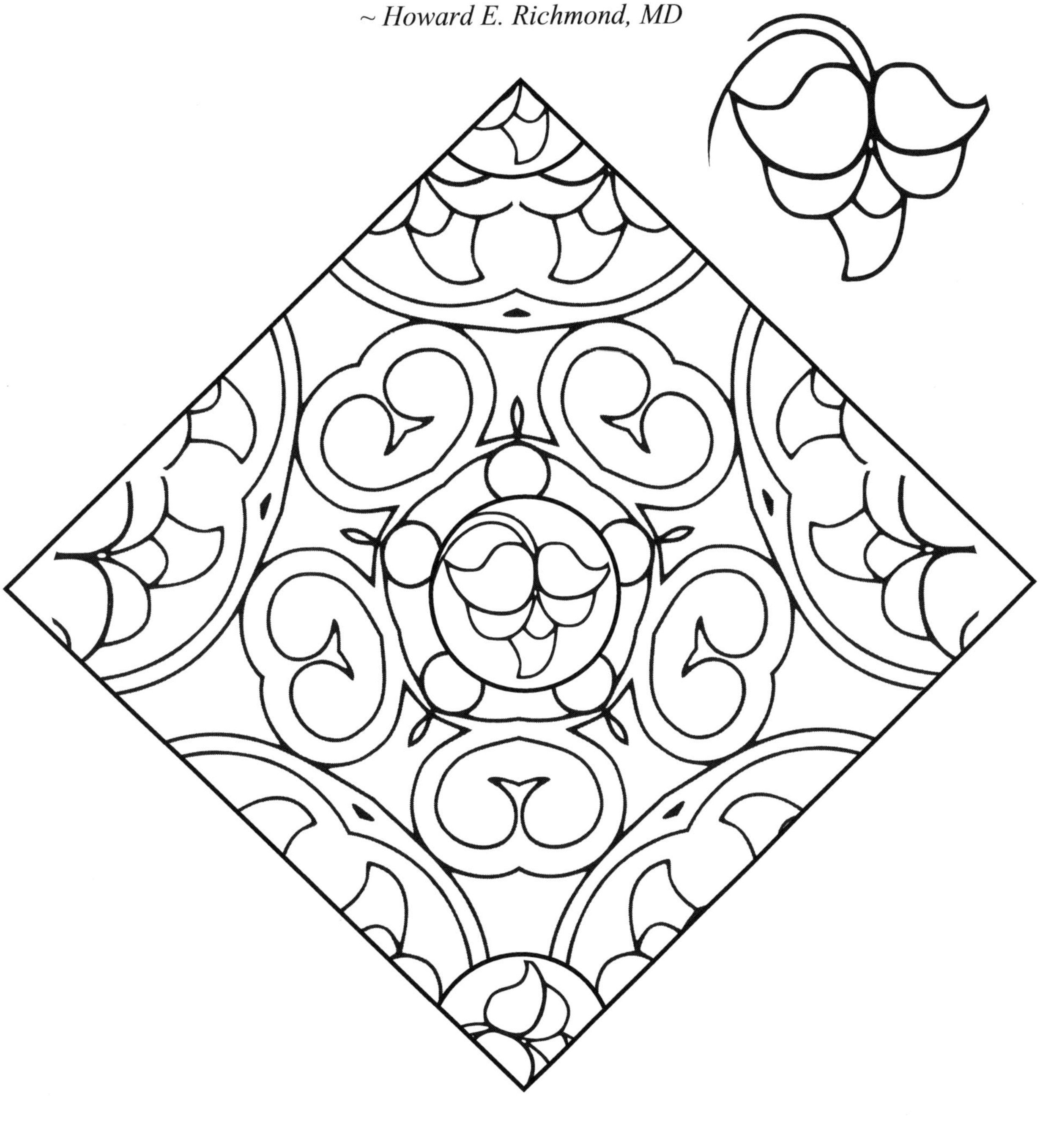

Rainbows & Chakra Colors – Some people like to equate colors with the Chakras, which are invisible "energy centers" throughout or bodies. They correspond with colors we usually see in a Rainbow -- from Red to Purple, with White being the highest color as it contains all colors. (Black is the absence of color, by the way.)

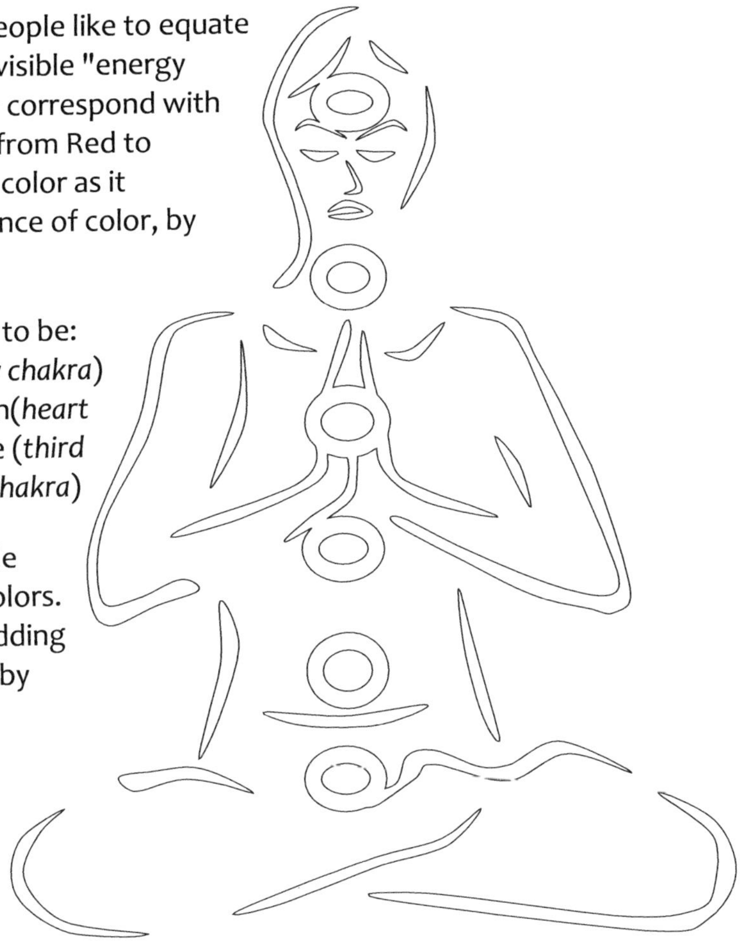

Chakra colors are usually considered to be: Red (*root chakra*) - Orange (*creativity chakra*) - Yellow (*power center chakra*) - Green(*heart chakra*) - Blue (throat chakra) - Purple (*third eye/intuition chakra*) - White (*crown chakra*)

Color hues are either primary (a single color) or a combination of primary colors. A SHADE is a color made darker by adding black. A TINT is a color made lighter by adding white. A color's VALUE depends on how light or dark it is.

Primary Colors – Red, yellow and blue are considered primary colors -- singular by themselves.

All other colors are blends of these three: orange = red + yellow; purple = red + blue; green = blue + yellow.

Shades and Tints – Pastels (tints) are light versions of primary colors or combinations; Shades are dark versions (primary or combination color plus gray, brown or black).

To easily make a Shade of a particular color, try coloring over a black line or section on our coloring pages.

Experiment with putting colors next to each other on our **Coloring Test Chart page** – even shades or hues you don't think might look good, like green and orange or purple and red. You might be surprised how good they can look in the right shades or tints or as accents (just a pop of color)! You can also outline a section in a darker or lighter color and fill it in with the same hue in a lighter or darker value.

You could use each color in your kit in one picture or only one color in different tints and shades!

(Source: *Wikipedia*, Color)

"COLORING TEST CHART" TO EXPERIMENT WITH YOUR COLORING TOOLS

We invite you to fill in our blank Color Chart page using the Coloring Tools you have at hand – gel pens, pencils, crayons, markers.

This can help you envision how your colors will show up on our coloring pages before you begin coloring -- then you will know your colors tints, hues and values, and can see how they might look next to other colors in your palette or if you mix them together.

© 2015 Coloring Books for Healthy Living

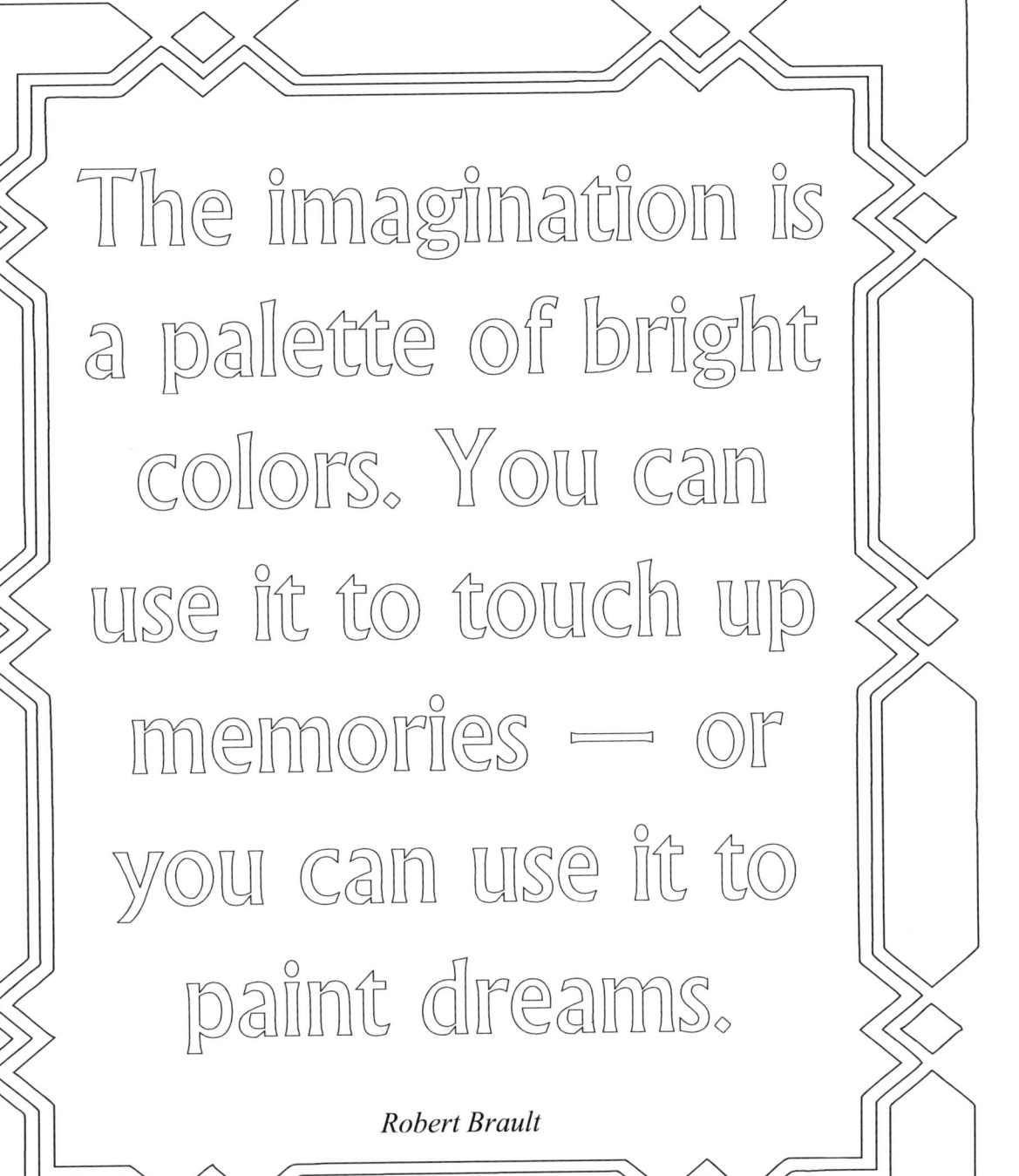

The imagination is a palette of bright colors. You can use it to touch up memories — or you can use it to paint dreams.

Robert Brault

WHAT'S INSIDE?

Interspersed with fun, beautiful coloring pictures, places to attach your "EMA™ prescriptions", places to journal and references to teachings and guided meditations, you will find....

Introduction
- Foreword by Dr H (Howard E. Richmond, MD ~ Creator of Emotional Martial Arts™)
- Letter from Elana
- Letter from Deborah
- Benefits of Coloring
- How to Use This Book
- Colors of the Chakras
- Color Test Chart

EMA Tools & Principles: each section has
- Emotional Martial Arts™ Topic
- Guiding Principles
- URL for teaching and guided mediation (HowardRichmondMD.com/Meditations)
- Places to journal and/or glue items
- Coloring mandalas

EMA Trainings

10/06/15 **Positively Not:** How to say no graciously in any situation–without guilt, shame or fear.

10/20/15 **The Art of Compliment Giving and Receiving:** Why it's hard to receive compliments and how empowering it is to give and receive them with grace and ease.

11/03/15 **From Survival to "Thrival":** A new language to embody consciousness In action (CIA).

11/17/15 **Weapons of Mental Destruction (WMDs):** How to diffuse anger arrows, guilt grenades, shame shrapnel and betrayal bombs.

12/15/15 **Sticks & Stones (Can Break Your Bones):** And words can harm or heal

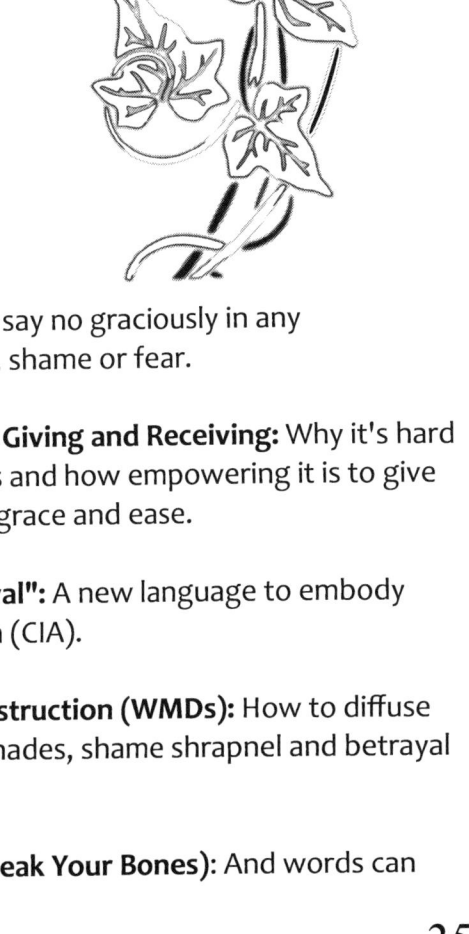

The 3 Committee Members

The 3 Committee Members in REACTION Mode

CHILD — vulnerable, approval-seeking

ADOLESCENT — angry, rebellious

PARENT — critical, judgmental

FEAR, SADNESS
Guilt, Shame
Worthless-ness

ANGER
Resentment, Jealousy
Betrayal

Thoughts, Beliefs
JUDGMENTS
Conclusions, Story

Copyright © 2015 by Howard E Richmond, MD

The 3 Committee Members in CREATION Mode

Joyful

Loving

Accepting

Aligned

Integrated

Present

Creative

Compassionate

CHILD — wondrous, creative, playful

ADOLESCENT — engaged, enthusiastic

PARENT — unconditionally loving

Emotional Martial Arts™ // HowardRichmondMD.com

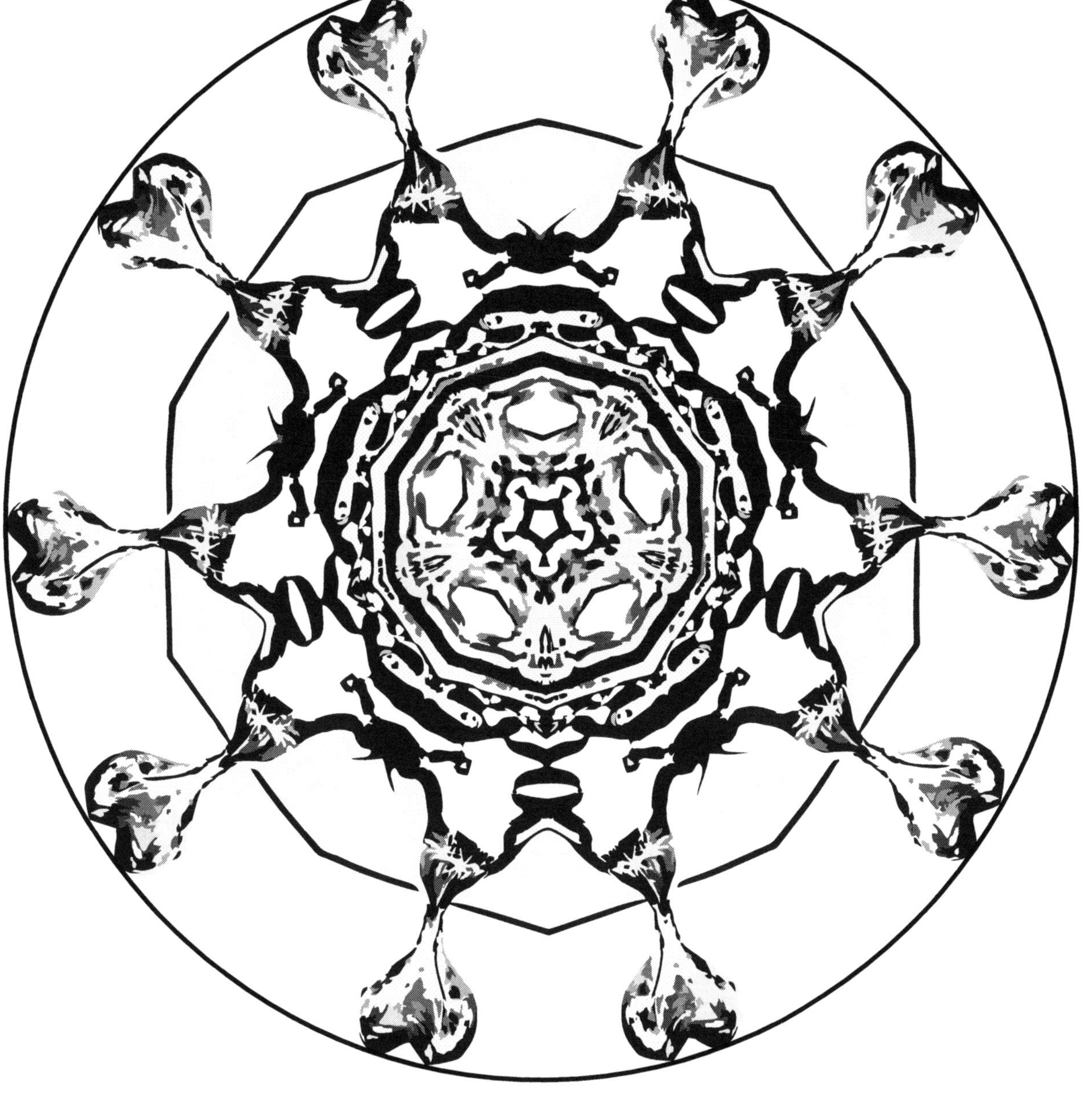

Black Belt Tools *HowardRichmondMD.com/Meditations*

Positively Not: How to say no graciously in any situation.

Do you say NO when you need to say NO? Do you avoid saying NO? Do you say NO with excess aggression or other emotion? Are there certain people or situations that make it more challenging for you to say NO? Are there times you say YES when you really want to say NO?

1. Observe the stories, thoughts and beliefs around these answers. Recognize these stories are judgments in disguise. List the judgments.
   _____
   _____
   _____

2. Mentally set aside the stories in the "judgmental parking lot," to give yourself some space between these thoughts. (These stories are typically generated by the **"judge"** or **"critical parent"** in the "Committee of 3".)

3. Cultivate the **Non-Judgmental Observer** (**NJO**) in you by practicing releasing any judgments about your judgments. (This action gets your **critic,** or **judge,** off the "throne.")

4. Do a full emotional inventory starting with the **"child."** Recognize the presence (or absence) of fear, sadness, guilt, shame and/or worthlessness. Name each emotion that is present, no matter how big or small the emotional charge is.
   _____
   _____
   _____

5. Do a full emotional inventory of the **"adolescent."** Recognize the presence (or absence) of anger, resentment, jealousy and/or betrayal. Name each emotion that is present, no matter how big or small the emotional charge is.
   _____
   _____
   _____
   _____

~more~

6. Validate the presence of each emotion by practicing releasing any judgments you may have about these emotions. This process: **R**ecognizing, **V**alidating, and **R**eleasing (**RVR**) emotional tension… requires practice, persistence and patience – and continued cultivation of the **NJO**.

Three Key Points or Attach EMA Prescription here:

1. Recognize & Release the judgments that drive you to avoid saying "NO"

2. "RVR" the emotions that drive you to avoid saying "NO"

3. Practice the delivery of your truth/message with calm empowerment

HowardRichmondMD.com/Meditations

35

Black Belt Tools   *HowardRichmondMD.com/Meditations*

The Art of Compliment Giving & Receiving: Discover the inner peace & grace of authentic acknowledgment of self and other.

Do you ever feel uncomfortable when someone gives you a compliment? Do you feel worthy? Do you crave receiving compliments? Can you give compliments with ease? Do you ever give compliments to "get" something from someone? Is it challenging for you to give others compliments?

1. Observe the stories, thoughts and beliefs around these answers. Recognize these stories are judgments in disguise. List the judgments.

   _____
   _____
   _____

2. Mentally set aside the stories in the "judgmental parking lot," to give yourself some space between these thoughts. (These stories are typically generated by the **"judge"** or **"critical parent"** in the "Committee of 3".)

3. Cultivate the **Non-Judgmental Observer** (**NJO**) in you by practicing releasing any judgments about your judgments. (This action gets your **critic,** or **judge,** off the "throne.")

4. Do a full emotional inventory starting with the **"child."** Recognize the presence (or absence) of fear, sadness, guilt, shame and/or worthlessness. Name each emotion that is present, no matter how big or small the emotional charge is.

   _____
   _____
   _____

5. Do a full emotional inventory of the **"adolescent."** Recognize the presence (or absence) of anger, resentment, jealousy and/or betrayal. Name each emotion that is present, no matter how big or small the emotional charge is.

   _____
   _____
   _____
   _____

~more~

6. Validate the presence of each emotion by practicing releasing any judgments you may have about these emotions. This process: **R**ecognizing, **V**alidating, and **R**eleasing (**RVR**) emotional tension… requires practice, persistence and patience – and continued cultivation of the **NJO**.

Three Key Points or Attach EMA Prescription here:

1. Recognize & Release judgments about giving or receiving compliments

2. "RVR" the emotions (that may be hidden)–e.g., guilt, shame and/or worth-lessness

3. Practice accepting & giving compliments with increasing self-confidence & ease

HowardRichmondMD.com/Meditations

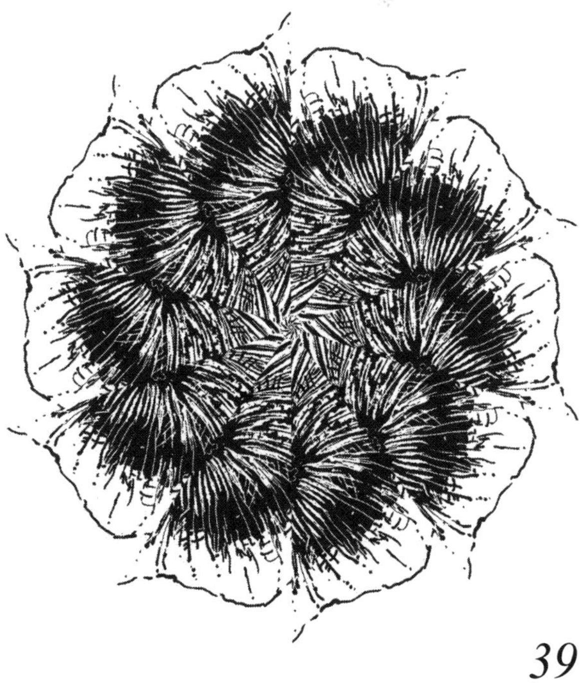

There is nothing
to fix or solve ...

just an
opportunity
to evolve.

Howard E. Richmond, MD

Black Belt Tools HowardRichmondMD.com/Meditations

From Survival to "Thrival": We can get out of survival mode and practice this new language embodying consciousness in action.

Do you ever feel overwhelmed by aspects of your life? Do you ever feel weighed down by the past and worried about the future so you are barely present in the now?

1. Observe the stories, thoughts and beliefs around these answers. Recognize these stories are judgments in disguise. List the judgments.
   _____
   _____
   _____

2. Mentally set aside the stories in the "judgmental parking lot," to give yourself some space between these thoughts. (These stories are typically generated by the **"judge"** or **"critical parent"** in the "Committee of 3".)

3. Cultivate the **Non-Judgmental Observer** (**NJO**) in you by practicing releasing any judgments about your judgments. (This action gets your **critic,** or **judge,** off the "throne.")

4. Do a full emotional inventory starting with the **"child."** Recognize the presence (or absence) of fear, sadness, guilt, shame and/or worthlessness. Name each emotion that is present, no matter how big or small the emotional charge is.
   _____
   _____
   _____

5. Do a full emotional inventory of the **"adolescent."** Recognize the presence (or absence) of anger, resentment, jealousy and/or betrayal. Name each emotion that is present, no matter how big or small the emotional charge is.
   _____
   _____
   _____
   _____

~more~

6. Validate the presence of each emotion by practicing releasing any judgments you may have about these emotions. This process: **R**ecognizing, **V**alidating, and **R**eleasing (**RVR**) emotional tension… requires practice, persistence and patience – and continued cultivation of the **NJO**.

Three Key Points or Attach EMA Prescription here:

1. Recognize how often we get triggered & stay in "reaction" or "survival" mode

2. Use the tools of EMA to RVR emotions & judgments that keep us stuck in survival/reaction

3. Experience the release of tension and the joy & empowerment that accompanies being in "thrival" or "creation" mode

℞

HowardRichmondMD.com/Meditations

47

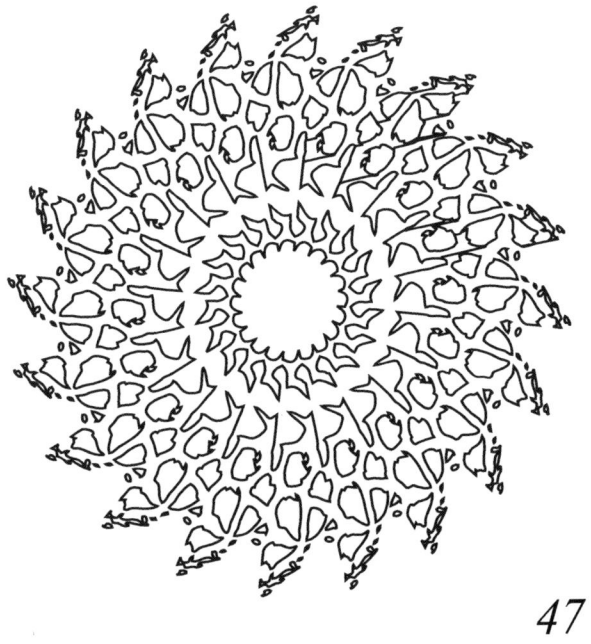

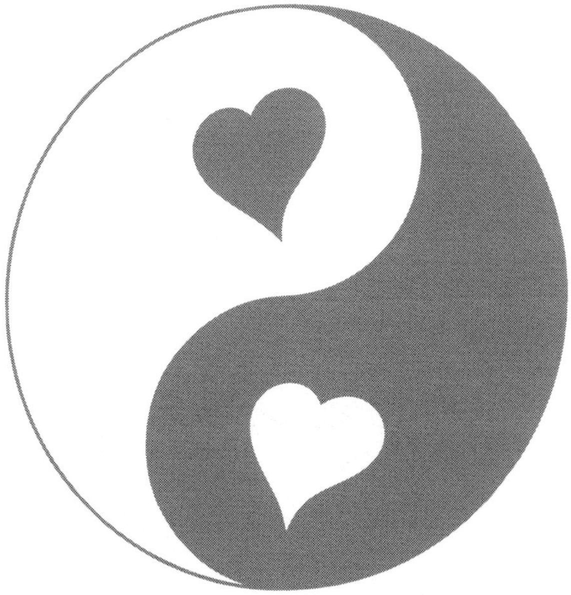

Black Belt Tools

HowardRichmondMD.com/Meditations

Weapons of Mental Destruction (WMDs): What they are and how to diffuse them.

Have you ever been a victim of WMDs ("weapons of mental destruction"), such as anger arrows, guilt grenades, shame shrapnel, betrayal bombs, passive-aggressive powder, etc.? Have you ever used these WMDs on others?

1. Observe the stories, thoughts and beliefs around these answers. Recognize these stories are judgments in disguise. List the judgments.
   _____
   _____
   _____

2. Mentally set aside the stories in the "judgmental parking lot," to give yourself some space between these thoughts. (These stories are typically generated by the **"judge"** or **"critical parent"** in the "Committee of 3".)

3. Cultivate the **Non-Judgmental Observer** (**NJO**) in you by practicing releasing any judgments about your judgments. (This action gets your **critic,** or **judge,** off the "throne.")

4. Do a full emotional inventory starting with the **"child."** Recognize the presence (or absence) of fear, sadness, guilt, shame and/or worthlessness. Name each emotion that is present, no matter how big or small the emotional charge is.
   _____
   _____
   _____

5. Do a full emotional inventory of the **"adolescent."** Recognize the presence (or absence) of anger, resentment, jealousy and/or betrayal. Name each emotion that is present, no matter how big or small the emotional charge is.
   _____
   _____
   _____
   _____

~more~

6. Validate the presence of each emotion by practicing releasing any judgments you may have about these emotions. This process: **R**ecognizing, **V**alidating, and **R**eleasing (**RVR**) emotional tension... requires practice, persistence and patience – and continued cultivation of the **NJO**.

When we commit to nonviolent communication, when we stop using WMDs on others, we no longer attract it.

Three Key Points or Attach EMA Prescription here:

1. Become proficient in recognizing & articulating the WMDs

2. Discover where, when & how you get triggered and become a victim or victimizer of WMDs

3. Practice & appreciate the difference between diffusing & detonating the WMDs

℞

HowardRichmondMD.com/Meditations

53

55

Black Belt Tools   HowardRichmondMD.com/Meditations

Sticks and Stones (Can Break Your Bones): And words can harm or heal.
Discover specific word choices to make instantaneously ~ to empower you.

Do you find yourself commonly using the word "should?" Like, "I should have done this" or "I should have done that?"

1. Take a moment and write down some examples specific to you.
   _____
   _____
   _____
   _____

2. Check your breath as you read these sentences to yourself and notice if there's tension in your body.

3. Now rewrite your sentences and replace "should" with "could."
   _____
   _____
   _____
   _____

4. Notice if there's a release of tension in your body as you read these sentences to yourself.

The word "should" has hidden, and often toxic, judgment. "Should" implies you or someone else failed; and we either condemn ourselves or someone else. Replacing "should" with "could" releases judgment and opens the pathway for healing.

When we practice noticing how often we use polarizing, limiting or judgmental words (e.g., good/bad, right/wrong, always/never, etc.) and then practice replacing judgmental language with nonjudgmental words, it allows us to shift our energy from tension to ease.

~more~

Three Key Points or Attach EMA Prescription here:

1. Practice "but" removal & replace with "Yes….and…"

2. Recognize the limitation of polarizing words–e.g., good/bad; right/wrong; always/never; etc.

3. Replace polarizing & limiting words–e.g., can't, should, easy/hard–with EMA language that's neutral & inclusive

℞

HowardRichmondMD.com/Meditations

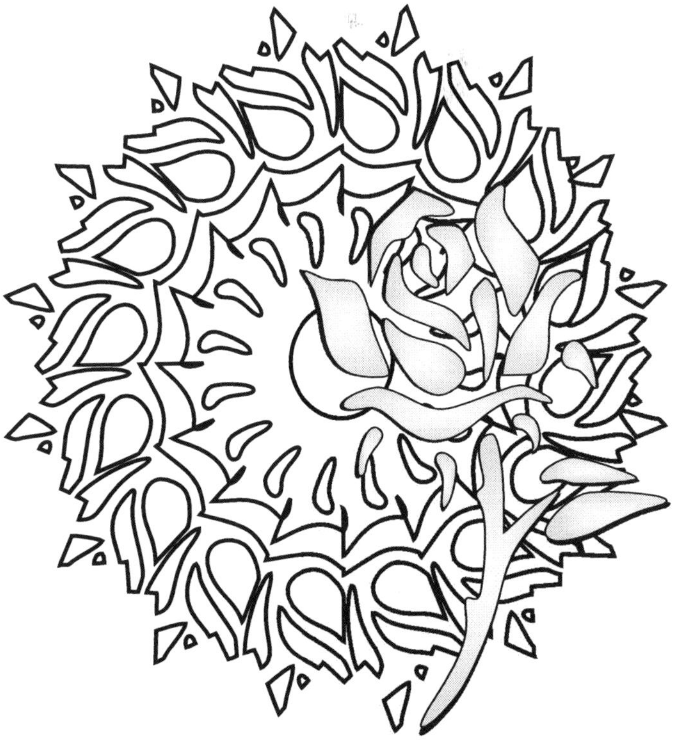

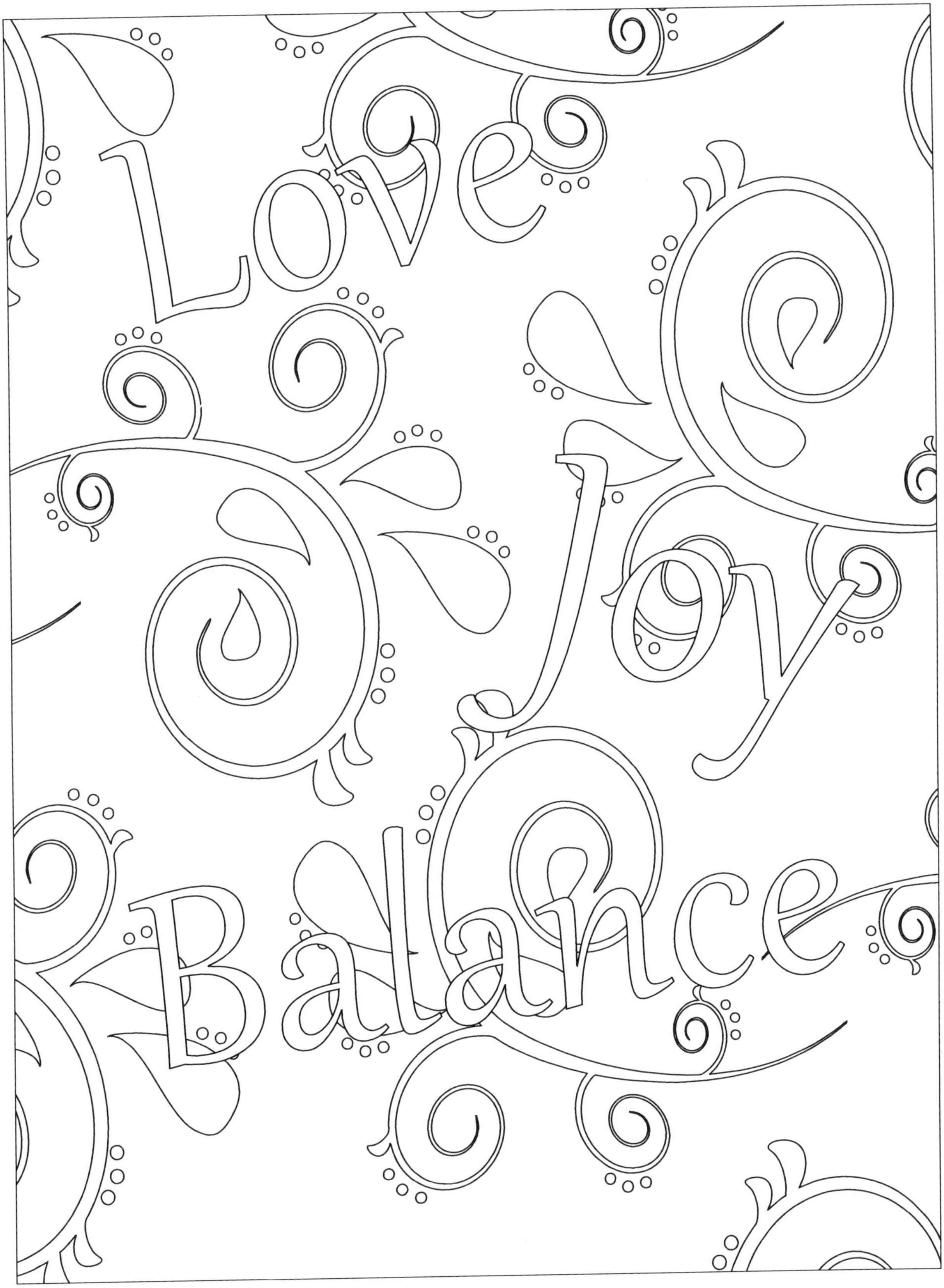
Love
Joy
Balance

Emotional Martial Arts Coloring Journal (Volume 1)
The Authors

Elana Cohen Richmond

The death of her father as a child uprooted Elana and her family from the Midwest to the south – where she felt like a fish out of water. As a result, Elana learned to swim on her own terms in different waters – whether as a waitress, a corporate executive, real estate broker, business manager or clinical care coordinator for a psychiatric practice. No matter the "ego costume" she wore, Elana developed three guiding lifelong spiritual questions: 1) "Will this be important when I get to the end of my life?"; 2) "How can I experience my daily activities as the expression of my spiritual essence?"; and 3) "How can I make it fun (otherwise, there's no point)?"

Deborah Louise Brown

With over 30 years' experience as a publicist, marketer, editor, publisher, promotional consultant, freelance commercial writer, and speaker, Deborah Louise Brown is a consummate collaborator and co-creator. She operates a boutique firm that provides marketing, platform-building, editing, graphic design, and publishing for authors and entrepreneurs. She assists authorpreneurs with editing and formatting their books and crafts strategies for topping the Amazon best-seller lists. In addition to writing a series of marketing books and trying her hand at cozy mysteries, Deborah designs, illustrates and markets coloring book journals for adults and children.

Emotional Martial Arts™ Series 2015

Howard E. Richmond, MD

WHEN: Two Tuesdays Each Month ◆ 6:30 PM – 8:00 PM
WHERE: California Institute for Human Science
701 Garden View Court, Encinitas

Please bring a pillow or mat or whatever you need to be comfortable.

07/07 The Story Beneath the Story: How emotions drive our perception and shape our reality; how emotions hide; and how emotions don't know the calendar.

07/28 The ½ Golden Rule: Why doing unto others is not enough and how doing unto self makes us whole.

08/18 Being Vulnerable and Empowered: How these two states can co-exist and why both are essential for personal growth.

09/01 Sticks and Stones (Can Break Your Bones): And words can harm *or* heal. Discover specific word choices to make instantaneously–to empower you.

09/15 The Intersection of Ego & Spirit: Experience how to cultivate the sacred space where transformation takes place.

10/06 Positively Not: How to say no graciously in any situation—without guilt, shame or fear.

10/20 The Art of Compliment Giving and Receiving: Why it's hard to receive compliments and how empowering it is to give and receive them with grace and ease.

11/03 From Survival to "Thrival": We can get out of "survival" mode and practice this new language embodying *consciousness in action*.

11/17 Weapons of Mental Destruction (WMDs): How to diffuse anger arrows, guilt grenades, shame shrapnel and betrayal bombs.

12/15 Judgment is a Truth Contaminant: When we are in judgment we do not value other points of view. Discover the gift of releasing judgment.

A $10 Donation is Appreciated. Your donation benefits The Healing Field Foundation, dedicated to strengthening individuals and communities in the practice of waging inner peace.

Inner Peace ... Wage It!

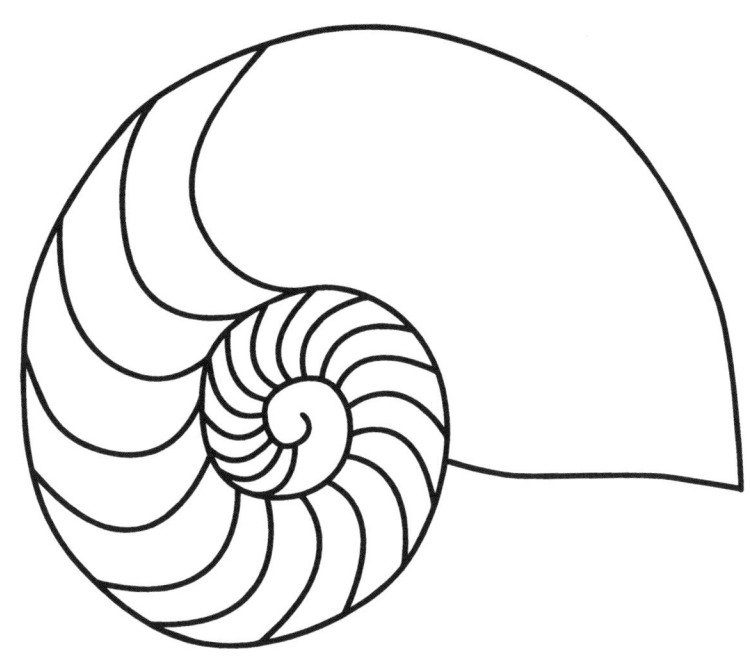

Emotional Attunement for Sound Relationships

WHEN: One or Two Wednesdays Each Month
6:30 PM – 8:00 PM

WHERE: California Institute for Human Science
701 Garden View Court, Encinitas

DATES in 2015

- May 13
- June 10 & 24
- July 15
- August 5 & 26
- September 9 & 30
- October 14 & 28
- November 11
- December 9

Howard E. Richmond, MD and an experienced team of sound healers will lead a guided sound meditation journey into emotional healing and beyond.

Dr. H will gently guide you into enhanced emotional awareness and release to improve relationships with self and others and bring more joy into your life.

We recommend you arrive 15 minutes early to get settled in. Please bring a pillow, mat, eye pillows and whatever makes you comfortable. We have 20 yoga mats and free water for people.

A $10 Donation is Appreciated.
All sound healer performances benefit the Bishwa Seva Foundation. Bishwa Seva is a 501(c)3 trust, formed to educate disadvantaged kids in Nepal.

HowardRichmondMD.com

THE
Healing Field
A Young Psychiatrist's Battle with His Anorexic Patient, Her Hunger Strike against God, and Their Journey through the Dark Night of the Soul
"Beautifully crafted and gorgeously delivered composition based on a real life story"
—Wendy Behary, LCSW
Disarming the Narcissist
Howard E. Richmond, M.D.

HowardRichmondMD.com/book

NIEA
WINNER
NATIONAL INDIE EXCELLENCE® AWARDS
FINALIST
GOLD

Transformational psychiatrist and author Howard E. Richmond, MD is an inspirational teacher and transformational coach who greets people at the intersection of body, mind and spirit and guides them to live the best life imaginable. His lessons about releasing judgments and hidden emotions introduce a new language that fuels and stimulates personal growth. One of the lessons he's learned over twenty years in private practice is the value of being "out of your mind" and into your heart. *The Healing Field,* his first novel, is a riveting account of the healing breakthrough that saved his anorexic patient's life and transformed his own. Richmond practices hot yoga daily in San Diego, California, where he lives with his wife, Elana, and their two German shepherd rescues, Jayde and Houdini.

THE
Healing Field
Howard E. Richmond, M.D.

The Healing Field

A Young Psychiatrist's Battle with His Anorexic Patient, Her Hunger Strike Against God, and Their Journey through the Dark Night of the Soul

by Howard E. Richmond, MD

MindExpander Press, September 2014

ISBN: **978-1-49747571-7**

245 Pages, 5.5" x 8.5" softcover

ISBN: **978-0-9907462-0-1 Kindle**

Praise for *The Healing Field*

The Healing Field is more than a novel. It is a beautifully crafted and gorgeously delivered composition based on a real-life story. It thoughtfully reveals the bold and unabashed narratives of a psychiatrist and his patient amid their strengths and struggles, personal and conjoint experiences, and raw texture of authentic humanness. Narrating with a mellifluous and metaphorical voice, Howard Richmond offers readers a unique opportunity—inviting them to enter the private emotional residence of an unconventional treatment room. The book is respectfully and entertainingly written. Readers are permitted to peer into the personal world of a devoted physician and the complex challenges he shares from the confidential file folder of one woman who experiences a courageous awakening.

—**Wendy T. Behary**, LCSW, author of *Disarming the Narcissist: Surviving and Thriving with the Self-Absorbed*

The Healing Field is a riveting novel about the healing journey of doctor and patient—a universal story of how the power of love can conquer fear and make you want to live. Howard Richmond is the rare physician who knowingly crosses unconventional terrain, with creativity and empathy, in pursuit of saving his patient from self-destruction.

—**Bill O'Hanlon**, featured Oprah guest and author of *Do One Thing Different*

Dr. Howard Richmond has an extraordinary ability to share his wisdom and experience with his patients. He helps them with clarity, love, humor and great devotion. I've observed him lecture, teach and inspire his colleagues and the community for over two decades. In *The Healing Field*, we can clearly see how Dr. Richmond is able to support, guide and empower. It is a must read for anyone who is interested in seeing what the power of the human spirit can do in the midst of terrible emotional trauma. Kudos to both teachers: Lori and Dr. Howard.

—**Daniel Vicario, M.D.**, ABIHM Medical Oncology and Integrative Oncology Medical Director, U.C. San Diego Cancer Center Director, Integrative Oncology Program San Diego Cancer Research Institute

Dr. Howard Richmond takes us on a healing journey through a complex web of human emotions, replacing fear, anger, shame and hate, with love, hope, courage and strength. His compassion and endurance combined with humor, intelligently sweep us into a world where the impossible not only becomes possible but real.

—**Nina C. Payne**, Author of *Moments in Time*

Howard Richmond's book, *The Healing Field*, is a story for all of us. Dr. Richmond offers us a clue to spontaneous medical remissions and how they can occur in a single moment of surrender and trust.

—**Paul Brenner, MD, PhD**, author of *Buddha in the Waiting Room* and *Seeing Your Life Through New Eyes*

ABOUT COLORING JOURNALS FOR HEALTHY LIVING

Emotional Martial Arts™ Coloring Journal (Vol. 1) is part of the *Coloring Journals for Healthy Living* family.

They say a picture is worth a thousand words. And even if you can't draw a picture, you can color one! Thank you to Barbara Schiffman for her words about the benefits of coloring.

In our info-whelmed world – filled with distracting screens, to-do lists and demands from family, friends, career and life-in-general – finding time to focus, relax and recharge can be a challenge. To help you "take a pause" whenever you can, *Coloring Journals for Healthy Living* books and calendars are a low-effort and high-enjoyment way to de-stress, focus your mind and activate your imagination. When you do this, you naturally create inner and outer balance. Coloring or journaling a page can take as little as ten minutes – or as much time as you have. But be warned that once you get started, you won't want to stop!

Resources on Coloring Journals for Healthy Living

ColoringJournalsforHealthyLiving.com

Get free coloring pages, articles and resources about coloring, color usage and psychology, stress relief, journaling and life balance at our website:
ColoringJournalsforHealthliving.com/Resources

Recommended Books about Color

(most are available at Amazon or via our CJHL Amazon store on our website)

Discover Color: Through the 5 Senses and Beyond
by Susan Bacon Trumpfheller
order at pendulumdowsingproducts.com/Color.html

Color by Betty Edwards: A Course in Mastering the Art of Mixing Colors
by Betty Edwards

Tony&Tina Color Energy: How Color Can Transform Your Life
by Cristina Bornstein & Anthony Gill

Color Psychology: Profit from the Psychology of Color: Discover the Meaning and Effect of Colors
by Richard G. Lewis (Kindle only)

Made in the USA
San Bernardino, CA
19 April 2018